let

Chloe Lorange

BookLeaf Publishing

Presentation by *BookLeaf Publishing*

Web: www.bookleafpub.com

E-mail: info@bookleafpub.com

ISBN: 9789395784375

First edition 2023

DEDICATION

for all the women in my life

and for those who struggle to find the words
sometimes

(also, hi mom!)

ACKNOWLEDGEMENT

i would like to thank Instagram for showing me this ad about a writing challenge. you're the boss.

on a more serious note, i want to thank everyone who inspired me to write this book.
i would like to thank my parents for adopting me and giving me a chance at life.
i would like to thank my two brothers and my sister for supporting me in all my projects.
i would like to thank my best friend for reading EVERY POEM i wrote (i love you halfsmores!)
i would like to thank my coaches for teaching me more than just gymnastics.
also, special thanks to all the authors who wrote a book i once read.

and to everyone who believed in me and keep believing in me, thank you.

LETTERTOMYSELF

dear me
life is shit
life is hard
but don't give up yet

someone once told me
when life gives you lemons
make the best lemonade ever
or just throw the lemons at them
it's funnier this way

a letter to myself
write about life
write about small things
write about love
about friendships
and strangers
write about life-changing moments

speak out your truth
you are more than what you think
speak up
open up
write and write
be vulnerable

they might not understand
but you will
create stories
or reveal reality
do as you wish
the pages are empty
fill them up
and leave them full of words

you waited a long time for this
so don't be afraid
throw them the lemons
and laugh at life
with all your heart
and love

dear me
do the best you can
life might be shit
but at least you can write about it.

AU

at first i didn't notice
walked right past you, didn't see the tears
coach said we were like sisters
for better or for worse
saw the pain in your face
shoulders shaking, heart crying
what happened, what's wrong
one word and i knew

the pain you felt
this feeling of sinking in the water
tidal waves, flow of disappointment
thinking she should be the one lifting me up
yet she's the one filling this ocean of tears
and you can't breathe, because if you dare to
you'll end up filled with more water
and the burning sensation of salt ripping your
lungs
and the weakness of your heart beating against
your chest

you ask for forgiveness for having such thoughts
for sinking by yourself
for not being strong enough to stand up to her
sorrysorrysorry

and your friends tell you to keep swimming
Nemo isn't real, but you keep dreaming
of a world where you can breathe underwater
without the ache of living
without the panic of hearing your name in her
mouth
without the danger of sinking in your own tears
without everything wrong that you did right.

but reality hits
as you look down at your innocent hands
and wonder, "what did i do to deserve this?"

i could say, "you don't deserve this" in a
thousand different languages
i could hug you a thousand times
but no one can make you swim
no one can make you breathe
more than yourself.

E

you said i was being disrespectful
for speaking to you that way
do you think you are being respectful
for responding that way?

i'm no one
did you ever think that there was a reason
a truth
behind my actions?
that maybe
i was right
that my feelings are valid and that emotions are
real
i learned a lot from reading books
but it shows how you never read one

i just wanted to be somewhere safe
i just wanted to be happy
for once, maybe not all the time
i just wanted to get out of this hole and forget
but i always seem to go back to what hurts the
most

i don't need a reminder
that i'm not perfect
that i truly am an ADHD kid
and that maybe i'm not doing enough
i don't need someone else to remind me
that i have scars on my arms
and that i have spent a year trying not to open
them again
and that maybe i'm just not enough

i hope you know i'm trying my hardest
to not fall back
to not jump off the edge
to not scare you
i hope you know how hard i try
to make you love me
to make you believe in me
to be part of your life again
i wish you knew so much more

my love for your smile when you think i'm
being reckless

my love for your laugh when i get the right
amount of humor

my admiration for your late-night studying

my admiration for your perseverance since the
first smile

i wish you knew so, so much more
than what you see

if you're reading this
i hope i make you proud
i hope you found a way to understand me
but above all,
i hope you know how much what we have and
what we are mean to me.

I

inside my house there is a place
nightmares tilting, asleep under the influence
the world and its poison
one drink and a little bit of smoke
one dream and a little bit of hope
the world and its poison

choose your poison
look down at your hands
constantly shaking
and your mind
constantly overthinking
inside my house there is this place
dreams sleepwalking during daytime
and insomniac nightmares setting my brain on
fire at night

the next day they ask me how i am
imfineimfineimfine
is all my brain is able to say
because my brain is used to lying
my brain is used to manipulating
my brain protects and protects
my brain creates thoughts
when i'm not doing enough

my brain creates anxiety
when i'm alone in a crowd
my brain creates depression
when i hurt the ones i love the most

and i should love myself for being alive
for fighting back the emptiness in my brain
for stopping the fire that burnt my heart
for being clean for so long
but inside my house there is this place
where it all means nothing
because the world and its poison
the nightmares and its drunkenness
is the poison i choose
is the comfort i enjoy
is the hug i embrace
and sometimes i wonder

i wonder about who i would be
if i'd never let them in at first
if i'd just say no
and they would've gone away
or maybe they'd force their way in
again and again and again
nightmares filling me up
or maybe i'd still be innocent
i wouldn't have to love myself just for being
alive
i wouldn't have to see the scars every day

i wouldn’t be reminded of who i am everywhere
i wouldn’t need to smile so much
or cry too much

because inside my
house there is a
place filled
with
you
.

GIRL

run, girl, run
you're running out of time
the clock is ticking
let me possess your mind

don't try to resist
don't try to reach out
i see your hand shaking
trying so desperately to hold onto something
realistic
but i will tear you apart
i will make you do things you hate
i will make you kill everyone around you
including yourself
but first
let me turn you into someone stronger
the greatest
my favorite soldier
the devil itself

run, girl, run
and take out your bow
plant arrows in all your loved one's heart
look how beautiful you are

so light in this darkness
look how high you can fly
now close your eyes and feel it
your heart beating against your chest
how all my doing was worth it
how you should've trusted me earlier
because deep down
i know you love being a threat to humanity
i know you enjoy being a threat to yourself
how manipulating them is so satisfying
it's so addicting, isn't it?

run, girl, run
with your hand reaching out
so innocent, yet so brave
what a soldier
what a killer
what a sweet throat slasher
running for all the blood
running because you want more
an arrow in their mind
the benefit of the doubt eating them
you are my prisoner
you are a prisoner of the fallen ones
it makes you mad, doesn't it?
it makes you lose your mind, doesn't it?
so now
it's time for revenge

run, girl, run
charm them with that pretty smile of yours
lie in their faces because they deserve it
they will eat you alive
and steal what's yours
kill them with kindness
take out their hearts
they deserve to know how it feels
to live without a soul
with this excruciating pain
of being helpless

run, little humans, run
you're running out of time
i am madness
run because it's already too late.

T

you made this world ours
you made this world mine
painted its wall with all my favorite colors
and built it with your strong embrace

remember that night
in the middle of the street, when you held me so tight
that night when pain became too much to bear
that night when i thought no one would care
do you remember?
remember that call
in the middle of the night, when love took its fall
that call when distance couldn't meet the end
that call when i thought i'd never see your face again
do you remember?

i remember
all the times you saved me
all the times you answered
i remember all the time
i remember when i get a glimpse of the ocean in your eyes

i remember when i hold your hand in a busy
street
i remember when i hear your laugh at midnight
on the speaker
i remember when you take all my tears and turn
them into pure water
i remember

all the flowers in the world
could never replace the smell of our home
all the chocolate chips cookies in the world
could never replace the taste of your tongue on
mine
all the love songs in the world
could never replace the sound of your heart
beating for us
all the books in the world
could never replace the words we created in our
story

some romantics make love promises with a ring
some romantics make love promises by posting
but we know, we remember the times
we remember all the things that would never
replace us

in this world
i believe in love
i believe in you
i believe in us.

i love you.

BOTHOFYOU

there is so much you need to know
so much you're dying to know
but you know
i know you know

you know what happened
why i had to run away
why i had to give up
why i am not who i was anymore
why my smile seems forced sometimes
why i bite my nails until they bleed
why i can't sleep at night
you know
because you know me
you know what happened

(you saw them, did you?)

you've slowly become a witness
a witness to the aftermath
how life treated me
and how i treated life
i didn't care about a lot anymore
i didn't eat
i didn't smile

i didn't talk
i didn't sleep
i didn't live anymore
i wasn't a person anymore
i wasn't even just someone
i was a ghost
a lifeless body with scars
and bones to eat
a lifeless face with dark circles under its eyes
and a useless mouth
i was already dead

what happened
is that i died twice
just a little the first time
and a lot the second
i was losing a little bit of myself each time
as if the shell of my soul hardened itself over the
years
for pretending i was doing fine
for being so hard on myself
for going on even when my body hurt
for all the things you thought were bravery
and courage and motivation
and then one day
the shell of my soul cracked a little
a little more
and more

i tried to fix it the first time
until it broke again
until it couldn't hold itself anymore
can't you see the broken pieces trailing behind
me?
i am making a path out of every mistake and
every person i hurt

one day i had enough
i understood
and i took one of the broken pieces
and cut
to see if what's hiding inside myself
was worth living for
it took me years
to understand that i don't feel pain anymore

i became used to life
or life became used to me
this feeling of being immortal
like nothing could kill me
like nothing could make me feel pain
life was tasteless
and i had enough
and that's why i did it

(you saw them, did you?)

MY

numb to the point where
we don’t fucking care
what will happen to us
what could happen to us
if we take this chance and dive in
who would care?
about one person
about one girl who’s still in her teenage dream
about one human who’s constantly struggling
who would care?

so numb that it doesn’t make any sense
because we are so used to feeling
sometimes guilt, sometimes pain
today the blood tastes different
it’s another smell
smell of overcoming our insecurities and
sadness
all the hurt he caused, all the doors he closed
why the fuck do i feel numb after all this time?
there is no answer to our feelings
and no truce to our broken promises
this numbness, this hole in your heart
you got so used to it

as i look at you
and try to communicate with you
you don't hear my screams
you don't hear my words coming out of my
mouth
"you deserve so much better
than this after feeling of being used
than this after feeling of being tired
than this after feeling of being a regret
this world doesn't deserve you
and neither did he"

you deserve yourself
you deserve to build a new home for your heart
a shelter that only you can get in
and that can never break
you deserve the space to flourish into yourself
and discover all the possibilities life can bring
in this universe
we are numb
we are careless
humanity doesn't bother with sense
humanity doesn't hold the truth
you create your own truth
your own reality
and you can be your own person

so numb, but you're not alone
we carry the same weight everyday
and we will continue to support each other
no one might care about us
no one might help us
but i will be there for you
i will be us
if you need me to be
i will be every feeling that you're missing
until you find yourself

just find yourself.

MAE

what's a soulmate?
a soulmate is someone who will love you
no matter what
a soulmate is someone who will protect you
no matter what
a soulmate is someone who will tell you the
truth
no matter what
a soulmate is someone who isn't scared of you
ever

she's my soulmate
some people would say that she's "my person"
but i do believe in soulmates
inseparable humans born apart
but will never be torn apart
i don't believe in a lot of things in this world
i don't believe in any God
i don't believe in faith
i don't even believe in myself

but she does
and i do believe in her
i believe she is the one person meant for me
life can get in the way sometimes
life can be harsh
and things might not be perfect
but what we have
is perfect
what we share
is perfect

it's like holding the universe in one hand
so fragile, sometimes you might be scared of
breaking it
yet so heavy, sometimes you wonder if you can
still carry it
but the universe is the universe
it's always been there
and it won't go anywhere
even when you close your eyes for a second
even when you are angry at the universe
even when you blame the universe for making
life so difficult
the universe will stand still
and so will you

a soulmate is inevitable
someone will cross your path one day
and will light the rest of your journey

a soulmate will hear about your strange
nightmares
and will laugh with you until they become
dreams
a soulmate will see you in your worst moment
and will stay up late until you are at your best

what's a soulmate?
she is
she is because i know
i know she is always there
she knows i am always there
because we know we are
there is no explanation
there is no proof
a soulmate
is she
her
M

DOJA

you are nothing but
a fraud
a player
a person
you're not the man
just a player in your own playground
a child that never made it to the big ranks
a kid that keeps on dreaming for something else
someone who needs something bigger than
himself

bigger
than the whole world
maybe if he just closed his eyes for a second
and think about his actions
he would see the pain he caused
the torture he forced on you
all the blood wasted on that day
the overthinking, this feeling eating you inside
he knows what he did
he knows who he corrupted
he knows why he wanted this so bad
but he doesn't know what we think of him

he doesn't know that his face will never make it
on the news
but his face will haunt thousands of women
will eat alive someone's mind at night
and will burn someone's heart to ashes
and that person will never rise again
because of him
because he wanted to have this twisted guilty
pleasure

sometimes she will close her eyes and wonder
about the same things
she will keep on dreaming for something else
she will need to become someone bigger than
herself
because she thinks that's how she'll get out of
this nightmare
how to get rid of this dying smell
and those walls she built around herself
but she keeps on building
because she doesn't want to witness the next
time
because she thinks there will be a next time
she is convinced she's not strong enough to
protect her fragile mind
and that's why she decided to

fake it until she made it
strong on insecurities, weak on confidence

so many ups and downs, but she'll get out
you don't know, but when she closes her eyes
and wonder
she dreams about a new life
about another way things could've gone
and she tells herself that it could be worse
but it is worse
and it's getting worse
and there is no way to stop it
until there is a way
an unfaithful way
a harmful way
a terrible way
but she just wants
a way.

you are nothing but a fraud
a player
a person
who deserves nothing
and never deserved her
who will be stuck in his own playground
and will never make it to the big ranks
just a kid
dreaming in a nightmare.

ONE

just a simple smile
and a soft “hi”
we crossed paths a couple of times
and i didn’t know why
he was buying coffee everyday
or why he was spending money on low-quality food
sometimes a woman would be there too
and buy a coffee
and sandwiches and salads
and health-destroying snacks
little things that would barely keep someone alive

one day i asked him
why we became used to see each other so often
why his visit became a habit
why he seems to like this coffee so much
i knew it would be something sad
in a hospital
i knew i’d regret asking

then he told me
“i’m here for my children”
“twins”

"they were born prematurely"
"we should stay here for two more months"
a simple smile
filled with sadness
"we lost one."

the man with one daughter
didn't cry
didn't break down
he held his head high
with one coffee in his hand
the other hiding in his pocket
shifting from foot to foot
unsure about life
unsure about what to do
and i couldn't say anything
i couldn't find anything
the words wouldn't come out

he wasn't scared
he wasn't sad
maybe a little disappointed
that the life he had turned out this way
that he didn't get the happy beginning
that he was so powerless
that all he could do was to buy coffee
and be a witness to this tragedy

i wish i could've told him
that life will take a different route
that life will sometimes drift away
and that you're the one in the front seat
and that your wife is by your side
holding the steering wheel with you
you might lose some people on the way
no matter how careful you are
no matter how good of a person you are
no matter how much love you give
but the only thing you can control is your car
your hands on the steering wheel
and how you choose to spend time
put on the song you fell in love with your wife
put on the song you fell in love with life
put on the song that makes your worries go away
and look right ahead
how the view is beautiful
how the next stop will bring peace
how the next turn will be a new experience
the roads you take will never be straight
i wish they would take our taxes and fix them
but it doesn't matter
because the car will always drive forward
even with little bumps
and some snowstorms

to the man with one daughter
the strength you create
is making you the best driver
and when you wake up
look forward
and know that
your child is right by your side.

SOCIETY

they say it doesn't matter
that tomorrow will be better
but there's nothing more horrifying
than knowing what they're not showing

and i knew
it would happen
but i didn't know
it would give me a pen
space to write
and love to give
not into politics
just into what is right

free to say anything?
doesn't stop them from judging
free to live?
i heard gunshots, how can we be so naive?
how many more do you need
how many lives will you take
women, men and children
how much do you need?

they say, “we hear you”
but they never listen, do they?
yes, me too
yes, say their names
yes, her body her choice
yes, there is no planet B
and there is nothing that can replace
the irreplaceable
the lifeless bodies weighing on yours
when you go to sleep at night
you dream of something bigger
you dream of power
you dream of confidence and selfishness
this is just a cover
a story you love to tell
your dreams are nightmares
your dreams are our nightmares

while they are constantly dying
you are living
in this place uncovered of sense
why are you so blind?
there are people dying
and there are bodies swimming through the masses
sorry isn’t enough
when not only one but everyday has been rough
because of your inaction

you need to respect them
and learn about their pain
because it could be a great way
to start your day.

women have rights, kids deserve a non-violent childhood, we need a peaceful world

NOTMYBODY

i am not my body
i am more
there is more to myself than my eyes
and my dark hair
i am not my body
i am

a human
like everyone else
like you
i am a daughter
i am a sister
i am a friend
i am a woman with ambitions
i am so much more than my body

i am a little bit like my mom
sometimes nervous, always generous
i am a little bit like my dad
we share the same hair color, and the same
awkwardness
i am a little bit like my brothers
ambitious and determined
i am a little bit like my sister
intelligent and perseverant
(although i sometimes wish i'd be more like her)

i am the person i became
and the future i envisioned for myself
i am all the mistakes
and the greatness i created
i am my nightmares and my dreams
i am the devil that haunts you
and the angel that has fallen from the sky

i am not my body
but i wish you would see it
i wish you could see what's inside
the home i built
the emotions i feel
the life running through my veins
because

i am not my body
i am who i am.

YESTERDAY

until we meet again
i have something to say
i know this isn't how it was supposed to end
i know this isn't what we planned
i have something to say

yesterday you were the one meant for me
you were the perfect person at the perfect time
the one i needed
the one i waited for my entire life
until today

yesterday i was the one for you
i was the best possibility in this universe
i was your little miracle
i was perfect
until today

yesterday we were the infinity
nothing could break us
nothing could end us
nothing would be us
more than we were us
until today
until we meet again.

TODAY

until we meet again
i have something to say
i know this isn't how it was supposed to end
i know this isn't what we planned
i have something to say

the truth is
i don't feel so good
guilt is eating me inside
for thinking about it
my hands are shaking
and my heart is breaking

the worst part about this
is that i would still do anything for you
i would still want to be anyone for you
but it's not the wanting that is missing
because there is so many things i would want
for you, for me
but there is so little time
and so much to do
i want it so bad
i would break myself for you
but sometimes
wanting is not enough

wanting is just another reason
to let it go
wanting is just an excuse
to put it on hold
wanting is futuristic
even if you want it now
it might never happen
no matter how hard you try
no matter how bad you want it
no matter how angry or sad you are
i can give you my all
my best
but i'll still want more
i'll be hungry for more
and you will too
until today
until we meet again.

TOMORROW

until we meet again
i have something to say
i know this isn't how it was supposed to end
i know this isn't what we planned
i have something to say

yesterday you will meet me
and you will be confident
you will never look back
you will only look forward
all the things we will become
all the moments we will share
you are in love
you tell yourself
it can't get any better
until tomorrow

today you will still be in love
and you will still want me
but you will want her
her with all the time in the world
her with all the problems
her
but she won't be alive anymore
and i will not be the one you want anymore

you will want to have quality time
you will want me to be there
but all i could give you was a few hours
sometimes none
and you will start to resent me
because i will have priorities
and you won’t be the first one
or the second one
because i will spend more time
with things that you’d never spend time on
with things that you will never be able to
understand
because they were not priorities for you
because you are far ahead
and i’m still here
and i can’t be at two places
even for you
until tomorrow
until we meet again.

TOMORROWAGAIN

until we meet again
i have something to say
i know this isn't how it was supposed to end
i know this isn't what we planned
i have something to say

tomorrow you will resent me
and hate me
for not choosing you
for choosing myself
and you will think i'm being selfish
how could i not spend time with you?
how can i not make time for you?
we will argue
we will fight
about what's right
and what's wrong
you won't understand
but i will

i will hate myself for being selfish
for keeping you to myself
for not being able to be more
not being able to be someone you can love
i will hate myself for hurting you

for seeing the pain filling up your eyes
and hearing your heartbreak
when i can't be all the things in the world
when you realize that i'm not her anymore
and that she's gone
replaced by someone motivated for more

there will be heartache
and pain
and death
but we will still be us
two people who were meant to be
who defined us
just two people
who learned
and taught

until we meet again
there is so much i want to say
i know this isn't how it was supposed to end
i know this isn't what we planned
so here's to everything we never said
here's to the next time
we will meet again.

LETTERTOMYFUTURESELF

dear me
life is shit
life is so hard
but don't give up

i love you
i promise i love you
and i always will
you are strong
you are beautiful
you are capable of so many things

you overcame a lot
remember all the struggles you went through?
remember all the fights you had with yourself?
remember all the nights you stayed awake?
keep remembering
keep looking back
and inspire yourself

you are a model
you fought so much
to be alive today
to be able to breathe
and live
you deserve to live

you deserve to keep going
because you went there once
you went there twice
(i know)
but you made it out
and you flourished
like no one else could
when no one else understood
when no one else thought you'd grow up
you did
i want you to plan a life for yourself
i want you to figure out things
you hurt a lot of people
and made a lot of mistakes
but they still love you
and you healed

you don't have time to doubt yourself
or overthink too much
keep working
keep writing
keep building yourself
you deserve it

be passionate
be creative
be confident
but most importantly
be yourself
and be alive

dear me
life is shit
life is so hard
but don’t give up
for me.

Printed in the USA
CPSIA information can be obtained
at www.ICGtesting.com
LVHW020002161223
766479LV00005B/416

9 789395 784375